FACE UP

A Collection of Outlaw Poems

Suzanne Nielsen

Foreword by Alison McGhee

Accolades

"Face Up exists where we live and dream and tell our friends about the harmony and discourse of our days and nights. It is not only what we all should read but what, if we allow it to, reads us."

—Akmed Khalifa, author of *The Camel's Shadow Has Four Humps* and *City Suite: A Collection of Short Stories*

"Suzanne Nielsen's poems are peopled with wry survivors attending to their lives with purpose and humor. In these poems of tenderness and grit, sorrow is always accompanied by wonder."

—Jacqueline Berger, author of *The Gift That Arrives Broken* and *The Day You Miss Your Exit*

"This collection treads a curious step between the edge of Midwestern myth and history, secret profundities and the everyday coffee cups worthy of verse. Strolling through the moonglow, blue noise and questions of true identities and the wisdom of a tree house, this is an ink-stained blast of wonder and inquiry sure to spark delight…"

—Bryan Thao Worra, Lao Minnesotan Poet Laureate and author of *DEMONSTRA* and *Before We Remember We Dream*

"While the poems in Face Up don't shy from the grit—we encounter doomed relationships, PTSD, and addiction—it's not all hopeless. We empathize with the shattered and become participants. These are poems of a life lived."

—Flower Conroy, author of *The Awful Suicidal Swans* and *A Sentimental Hairpin*

Copyright © 2022, Suzanne Nielsen

All rights reserved.
No part of this publication may be reproduced, stored in, or introduced into a retrieval system, or transmitted, in any form or by any means (electronic, mechanical, photocopying, recording, or otherwise), without the prior permission of the publisher.

Requests for permission should be directed to
info@OlebBooks.com

333 Washington Ave. N.
STE 300-9029
Minneapolis, MN 55401
www.olebbooks.com

Edited by: Belo Miguel Cipriani
Assistant Editor: Jonathan Hiatt
Copyedited by: Ellen Morgan
Book Cover and Interior Design by: Erik Christopher
Author Photo: Sarah Pierce

First Edition

Printed in the United States of America

Paperback ISBN: 978-1-7323127-5-3
ebook ISBN: 978-1-7323127-6-0

Library of Congress Control Number: 2022937840

Dedication

Face Up is dedicated to the memory of Amy Winehouse, whose tragic integrity reminds me of the power and perils in truth-telling, and that questions are far more seductive than answers.

"There's no point in saying anything but the truth." —Amy Winehouse

Contents

Accolades	2
Dedication	5
Foreword by Alison McGhee	10
Born and Bred East of the River	11
Fists for Hands	13
The Musty Smell of Shelter	14
Nearsighted Tree	15
Never Forget a Face	16
Midnight on the Midway	17
Resurrection	18
Patience	19
Window Shopping	20
Shattered	21
Listen to Me	22
Last Call for Depression	23
Prenuptials	24
Germs	25
A Less-Than-Purple Passage	26
The Sandbox	28
Freeze Frame	29
Timing Is Everything	30
Three Days Before the Witches Fly	32

Mapping Mama's Mind	34
Threadbare as a Habit	35
Twenty-Two Months	36
A Dog's Sense of Direction	37
Dickinson's Deed	38
The Width of the Foot	39
Twenty-Five Years of History	40
Matter of Fact	41
Pink Plugs	42
Strolling	43
A Mere Decade Plus Two	44
Bloodful Wills	45
Face Up	46
Bridge to Heaven	48
Raining from Heaven	49
Reading Lips	50
Minnesota Heat	51
Moonglow	53
Mental Health Update	54
Your Gut Response	55
News and a Cigarette	56
Empty Is a State of Mind	57
Face Painting	58
Enter to Win a Trip to Las Vegas	59
Atom and Eve	61
Blue Noise	62
True Identities	63
Have a Home	65
Translocation	66
Tree House	67

Another American Invasion	68
Consequences of Dawn	70
Such Colorful Stories	71
Filling My Mother's Shoes	73
Forty Percent Lost	75
Hoops	77
Excuse Me	78
37 Seconds	79
Profile of a Poet	80
Acknowledgments	82
About the Author	83

Foreword
by Alison McGhee

Long ago, a young woman sat tense and quiet in my creative writing class, head bowed, eyes on the table, holding tight to an internal world that would come tumbling out on the page. I still have a copy of *Eight Days*, the first story Suzanne Nielsen ever wrote in that class. The painful power of the friendship between two lonely, neglected children in that story was true of Suzanne's work then, and it is true of her work now.

A writer of compassion, urgent acuity, humor, and grit, Suzanne's new collection showcases her profound connection with the unsung citizens of our unfair world. Like a hummingbird, she dips briefly in and out of past and present. The raw power of a line like *I was born in the mid-fifties with fists for hands because in utero I knew life wasn't fooling around* is underscored by the raw pain of life with chronic depression: *For days I climb into bed wearing my street clothes that haven't seen the streets for weeks.*

The stark silence of an opening line like *I see on Facebook that my birth mother has died* is matched by the stark cancer humor of a line like *I can't wear a tank top because my top has tanked*. And then there are solitary poetic lines like *She walks with an accent, favoring her right side, but not enough to grieve equilibrium* and *the closet where two wire hangers with slender shoulders escape beneath the floorboards.*

Recurrent themes—physical and mental illness, life as an adoptee, the horrors of our political reality—are explored with the hard-won wisdom of middle age. Part fever dream, part calm reflection, *Face Up* is a memoir of a life lived intensely by a writer of her time who wields words both as weapon and medicine.

Suzanne Nielsen

Born and Bred East of the River

Follow the worn path to the maple tree in Nessen's front yard; listen to its stride
as the heron flies overhead. The blue overhead hovers just shy of your shoulders
as you memorize your surroundings just east of the river. This is your community
that embraces a dislodged memory as you stare at the palm of your hand. Look
beyond your reflection in water. Listen for the cues the ripples reveal.

Go back, remember the hesitation, perhaps a slap, someone is speaking, but you insist you can't enter a
story with dialogue. Sometimes you leave town to dance with dolphins until life says, "Come back," as you
ask, "How did I get here?" Anger writes endlessly in search of fictional identities which might otherwise
escape beneath the floorboards while the half-moon settles on a restful color of sand.

You once married to a man who obsessively washed his hands with diverted eyes, while another husband
overwound the Wittnauer, lips clamped like forceps on an infant's cranium
all recorded on surveillance cameras because you can't hide deformities behind the lens.

You hear the river; life ebbs and flows; you knew all along your DNA was a crapshoot. You reveal to
Winnicott your imposter syndrome, stare at the camera

Face Up

as he pulls a quarter from behind his ear. Just
above a whisper, your Little Pony metallic pink plugs sing you a story
as long as a stray hair the length of Rapunzel's. Your mind wiggles like Jell-O; you open the window,
shroud the clock, attend the open forum with Ned Rousmaniere to talk about grief
you can't take a break from, then depression gets pinched, and it's hard not to dwell in the hatred and
fear so I go back to the magical realm, where the sun glares through the sycamore, embraces your white eyebrow and inserts the key simultaneously as someone asks through a bullhorn if you are her, the girl
that got away.

Suzanne Nielsen

Fists for Hands

I was born in the mid-fifties with fists for hands because in utero
I knew life wasn't fooling around. Last night during my restless hours
I straightened my fingers and cleaned out my desk, a desk from the forties,
where I'd stashed a letter to myself in cursive fifty years earlier.
I inhale the half-century and drift back to its drafting under the weeping willow
that my father cut down when I left home. The retreat that bends its branches
for my teenage angst. There I sit, straw hat askew, nose in a book, pad and pencil
my company. We sit and share secrets wrapped in opiates, if you talk,
talk only to yourself because life isn't fooling around.

The Musty Smell of Shelter

It hurts you to talk about it,
but it hurts you more to not talk about it,
or
is that therapy gibberish?
To replay pretend discussions
in your head as you follow the path
past the musty smell of your family tent,
your kerosene stove,
latrine residue,
you pick blueberries in the sunshine
while swatting horse flies
as sweat stings your tear ducts.

After your stomach is full,
when you feel berry-drunk
or sun-bleached dry enough
to talk about
it, it
no longer exists.
Run into the lake,
slip and slide across slimy stones
until the water reminds you to hold it in,
hold your breath until you hit bottom.

Once a long time ago,
people never thought about talking,
only the primitive nature of feeling full
off of venison and hickory coffee.
Those days remain undocumented as a result,
but the pretense lingers behind submerged eyes.

Suzanne Nielsen

Nearsighted Tree

The maple tree in Nessen's front yard is the color of cranberries,
and just today it shed several of its leaves, some left swirling and
flying into neighbors' yards, where three children under the age of
ten jump and swing from the rope hanging on the lower branch.
They crash and land and laugh and bury one another beneath
a crimson blanket before it's time to go inside for supper,
and all rest until morning, when the tree,
in spite of being nearsighted, casts its
shadow over the backyard, left hushed.

Never Forget a Face

The heron flies overhead, taking the 10th Street exit into St. Paul
in unison to the mourning dove landing on the viaduct just east of the river.
Herons, I hear, never forget a face; they know if a smile is congruent with a heart,
if the wind is conducive for flight, and most importantly they know
humidity is brought on by caging anything capable of breath,
shallow and rhythmic, waiting to be left undisturbed
until the face is now a stranger.

Suzanne Nielsen

Midnight on the Midway

Bertha sat glued to the TV screen
as the Midway emptied out,
sending the debris of 3.2 drunks
slurring up to the window
to gawk at the fat lady and spit in her face,
then laugh in disgust.

Bertha grabbed the can of Glade
Air Freshener and sprayed it in their
faces as they swore to get her back,
and she swore to sit on them,
and I swore to watch her back,
and we became best friends
for those ten days, Big Bertha and me.

Resurrection

On Good Friday twenty-eight years ago, she met her biological mother
at the county welfare office. She said she felt her while outside
leaning up against a cement building, smoking a cigarette.
The sun, tamed by tar clouds and sunglasses, an ashtray
the size of a toddler, the tap of her shoe against the sewer grate
below where she stood, all comforted her like a roomful of relatives
at a christening, a graduation, an Easter brunch.

A social worker for the county introduced them, two women,
one twenty-two, one forty-four, neither having seen the other since the
younger was three. She said she recognized a slight resemblance
in the knuckles of their fingers, in the way they both tugged at their
undergarments. Out of her jacket pocket, forty-four pulled what twenty-two thought
was a deck of playing cards. Michaellawrenceanitakathleenamyphyllisevelyn
face cards, full house, half sibs.

"Just like that?" I said, "She pulled out the stack just like that?"

She looked at me and said, "That's not all. Her current husband's name was Bingo."

Suzanne Nielsen

Patience

It's so American to go to the ballpark,
watch a game, and stand up during the seventh inning
to sing about Cracker Jacks and home runs
while the two overweight twenty-something men
seated directly in front of you argue about Guns N' Roses'
most poignant album. "Use Your Illusion."
Not quite the adjective I think of when eyeing the arguers.
Maybe poignant, maybe all-American sitting beside
your first love entering your sixth decade,
or is that pure luck? Regardless, you can't
put your arms around a memory.

Window Shopping

At first I didn't see the lining of her coat hit her calves in a frayed, frantic search
for cover just like I didn't notice her lipstick smeared across the palm of her hand,
like a coral stripe indicating free membership into a hostel, or maybe a fancy
hospital band color-coded in only a way that hospital people talk. She was sipping
coffee, or possibly tea, maybe a tinge of cinnamon schnapps to take away her stale
breath from not talking out loud but only to herself in the glass window
where her shadow rested.

Shattered

She walks with an accent favoring her right side
but not enough to grieve equilibrium. Not enough
to complain at work where she lines the books with clues
to the culprit. On Wednesday, the color escapes her face
as the books on 17A are boxed and burned.
It doesn't prevent her from color-coding future clues.
Once the code is broken she will need a new gait, another lift,
so to speak, before moving down to the river and abruptly
skipping stones. Water ought never be interpreted as glass.

Listen to Me

Toby Walker had listened to everyone
around him for his entire forty-three years. One
day he woke up and realized living in Taipei
proved healthy as far as diet was concerned;
however, he has never spoken Mandarin
and does not have any idea what people are saying.

"I look at their faces and that is my translation,"
he said in an interview. I reminded him what
Stein said so many years ago when living in
Paris: "Let me listen to me and not to them."

He had no idea what I meant. I watched him
walk away and noticed him searching the faces
of the strangers he passed. After passing a woman
with a lollipop, he turned to face me and was smiling.

Suzanne Nielsen

Last Call for Depression

Loren and Janeen Marie tossed back daiquiris at Schweitz's,
pocketing the drink umbrellas they'd sell when sober
to the delinquents down the street for a dime apiece.
The patrons next to them were resident dart enthusiasts,
and when asked to join in, Loren became reticent,
excused himself to the restroom,
but kept walking to the street curb, fondling his pocketful
of tropical designs until it started to rain, whereupon he
rendered their worth, put his head back, and took
communion from above.

Prenuptials

It didn't hit me until a decade into my fourth
that I'd had three bad marriages
before the age of forty.
If I start configuring this into dog years,
it may be that I'm quite the bitch,
or the runt of the litter, depending.
I want to believe my bark
is worse than my bite
and rabies shots are only
for the neutered
and honky-tonk women.

Suzanne Nielsen

Germs

The doctor tells her, after thirteen weeks in a cast,
her son's wrist needs surgery,
then eight more weeks in a cast, minimum.

They will take bone from his hip,
connect it to the wrist bone
that's connected to a night in the hospital.

She calls her ex to let him know,
not that he's entitled, she's got sole
legal and physical custody;
she does it for selfish reasons.
Her son needs a ride to the hospital.
Her sick days are used up,
and she's tired, the ex retired.

The ex wants her to call the doctor
and remind him to wash his hands
before surgery. Many medical people
don't wash their hands enough, he says,
including doctors, he says. "I was a medic
in the army so I know this firsthand."

She gives the ex the phone number for the doctor's office,
suggests he call and voice his concerns.
If you get a voice mail, she says, leave a message
reminding them all to wash their hands
before surgery as I washed my hands of you.

A Less-Than-Purple Passage

My son is excited
for an eleventh grader
this is big
for him this is monumental
He is ordinarily stoic
and always in command
of his emotions

"What's this excitement about?"
I ask with sincere anticipation

I've been accepted to Annapolis's
summer naval academy program, he answers, eyes averted

He's pivoting with pride, delight, puritanism
at its finest. All those years I spoke out against
militarism, served on the steering committee for WAMM
reminding him that his uncle would have gone to Canada
instead of serving in Vietnam,
reminding him that his grandfather
received a purple heart in WWII
and never let go of the nightmares
died too young
a heart
broken from bloodshed
while a less-than-purple passage
remains
next to a flag precisely folded
in the shape of a dagger

Suzanne Nielsen

I want to scream from
the battlefield right out our front door
"War is here among us!"
Annapolis is not privy
to my eleventh grader
all the while he
the one with diverted eyes
remains in command

The Sandbox

At the eleventh hour of dwindling daylight, Saber Strike's javelineer Rocky Laurentsen
checks the command launch unit's infrared cameras, preparing for darkness to capture
the dead of night.
Nearly fifty pounds of gear digs into his right shoulder. The timid yet determined warrior's medium frame
reveals his camouflaged calluses to Julius Yego's javelin-throwing arms.

We're both so far from the sandbox we once knew, where over there, to the right lay
little green soldiers dreaming of purple hearts and to the left lay muscle men
spitting gold medals.

Perspiration puddles behind Rocky's neck, the missile launches,
summons the sky, surveying over 8,000 feet. An Olympian medal follows in its wake. Mouths agape, the funnel's infinite ghost gone.
Rocky clutches the dirt beneath his shaking frame, so damp.
Exhale.

Granules make their way to the launching pad, where giant clattering hooves prepare to
confer that warriors, all warriors mind you, know their playing field; all warriors prepare
to pause for eternity.

Suzanne Nielsen

Freeze Frame

How many mornings
has the sky warned me
to carry an umbrella
So I married a man
who'd never owned
an umbrella
He'd never owned
a camera. . . . Of course
I didn't know this
when I met him
I didn't know this
until four years later
when we were arguing
about the foreboding sky.
The sky, too, gives warnings,
I said. He just looked at me
and reached up, grabbed a piece
of that sky and said
this is how close we are to illusions
and this is why I will never
own a camera, an umbrella;
this is why, my dear wife,
meteorological observations
are negatives in a captured frame
that make the sky want to cry.

Timing Is Everything

My husband wants a manual-wind wristwatch.
This is something I have an opinion about.
He's never gotten over Reagan being elected.
Time stopped then, and America has steadily regressed, except for that brief
resurrection during the Clinton years.

I have Aunt Lil's wind-up Wittnauer, given to her by the St. Paul Police Department
in honor of her husband's twenty-nine years of service.
Can't read the dial, my husband said. I need an extra large; chubby wrists.

Aunt Lil kept that watch in the built-in buffet, top center drawer, lined in its satin box
like the coffin she was buried in a decade ago. I remember her opening that drawer, retrieving that red box, and winding the Wittnauer. She'd watch the second hand go around the dial for a complete circle,
close the box back up, and tuck it safely in the drawer.

Click click click she'd go, off to the kitchen to brew egg coffee.

Tonight, I went on eBay and spent three hours bidding on a wind-up watch.
Before retiring, I won the auction.

A 1960s Helbros Invincible Manual Wind Watch, just in time for Easter.

Suzanne Nielsen

This morning, I took the Wittnauer out of storage, in a drawer covered with vintage half-slips and camisoles. I set the time for daylight saving, wound the watch, watched the dial go around once, and slipped it on my wrist. I smiled, thinking how timing is everything.

Three Days Before the Witches Fly

She would have turned eighty today, three days before the witches fly.
For a Christian, that was an odd landmark, but hers and her reminder that October 28th was
her celebrated day of birth. The year I was thirty, pregnant with my first,
married to a trickster, she hadn't talked to me for three months.
Scared I was being seduced into the occult,
typical of a wide-eyed Scorpio, lips still taut
from deep underground.

I closed all the windows this morning,
a deliberate move, as some witches might be on the prowl early
to avoid congestion. I sat at my computer while I let the dogs out to pee.
The frisky white terrier didn't return, even when I shook the treat can.
I must explain, she's a runner. Chases cars, especially large American models and trucks with loud
mufflers. Four years ago she bounced off the tire well of an '87 Olds four-door and survived, runs bow-
legged to prove it.

I called her name, first of all in neutral tones, then in panicked shrills. Made my
way down the back steps in my blue Westie pajamas to find the fence gate ajar.

Suzanne Nielsen

Damn witches, I thought. All this three days before my
doctoral defense, all this and
there she is sniffing the Democratic senate sign in my
neighbor's yard, still in her pajamas. My eyes fill
with tears. I call her name; she runs the other direction
but is stopped by the neighbor's fence. I bend
over to scoop her up and she licks my face.

We make our way back to the house, through the gate,
close it behind us, and climb the stairs, where the
other dog is fast asleep in the sun on the tile floor.
Not bad for an old broad, is what I hear her whisper in my
ear. I close my eyes.
Lips still taut, still in control, there she is seducing me
from underground.

Mapping Mama's Mind

"Close that rain, here comes the door!"
Mama yelled things like this at me
throughout her entire life, so when
she was dying and said,
"I wrote that in my mind for you to read in my journal,"
I didn't think she actually meant it.
The night of the morning she transcended,
I curled up with her journal
in the corner of her small kitchen
close to her spices.

Then it happened.

I opened her mind and traced her paths,
not recalling a word I'd read,
but having a perfect story in my mind
of what it said. She left me a map
of her last seven years: all bad luck
related to mirror reflections.
On her map she'd chicken-scratched the town of Outrage,
a destination she dwelled in like purgatory.

Outrage opened its doors and invited her in.
When my mama showed the least resistance,
it yanked her by the neck like forceps on an infant's
cranium and held her in its clutches
until her last breath. Her mind was
ever determined and demented
to get even.

Suzanne Nielsen

Threadbare as a Habit

I called for Timothy out of habit. It's only shy of six months since he
left without a forwarding address. I think of him, his snow-white hair,
cowlick dead center revealing his widow's peak, drenched with sweat the
last hours before the end. When wet it gleaned a baby blue hue, such a boy
who early on knew his sexual identity, would cling to a crucifix in spite of Florence,
the aunt who married Christ early in her twenties, a virgin like Mary with a traveling altar.

God loves all his children, she said while caressing her habit, threadbare, sent to her
from the address of the Pope. We are all deserving of contentment, she said, barely moving
her mouth as though there was something decadent about the idea. I tell her in life contentment
is as threadbare as her cotton habit, and the best one can hope for is a place of supreme solitude.
Are you there, my friend, warm to the touch, content in the thought that all that perspiration led to a contented end?

Twenty-Two Months

My husband moved out twenty-two months ago.
After the first twelve-month lease, he
signed yet another.
Today he told me he
signed for a third year.

I asked him when he was coming home.

He said we have issues.
"You need to get in touch with
your inner child like I have," he said,
then exhaled into the phone,
exhausted,
I suppose,
from having me ask
once again when
he was coming home.

Suzanne Nielsen

A Dog's Sense of Direction

Last night on Animal Planet
four dogs were rescued from Queens.
One was thought to be dead,
cold to the touch,
curled up in a fetal position
in an empty box.
The ASPCA twirled their cherry lights,
broke the speed limit,
and within minutes the dog was hooked
up to fluids. It did not have a detectable
heartbeat. Six months later the dog
had fully recovered and was adopted
by a family who named her Hope. This
morning a friend of mine woke up with
six months of sobriety. He might someday
get a dog for a companion. Until then
he will jingle his medallion in his pocket
and mimic a canine sense of direction.

Dickinson's Deed

Like a surveyor, he comes to my house insisting
I need an extreme backyard makeover.
"While you're at it, you could use a makeover, too,
hiding indoors like Dickinson is unbecoming," he says
pointing to my feet as they slide along
pavement in flat tortilla-shaped cardboard thongs.

This is my ex-husband talking, no longer on the deed.
No longer in need of housing, due to his winnings
on a lottery ticket purchased on 9/11 at 7-Eleven
last fall, three years after the traumatic tumble of the towers
that started my heart's collapse.

"I need to make over the last twenty years
of my life that you stole from under me
leaving me flat broke," but who needs
a surveillance camera for that?
Always yammering
never anything to say.

Suzanne Nielsen

The Width of the Foot

Although she didn't request an RSVP, she expected to get a response
to a desperate call, an intervention so to speak, with the one who
remains speechless; after all those years of appearing as a couple,
after all the adapting to maniacal moods and idiosyncrasies
left dormant for significant periods of time, the truth reveals itself.

You can't keep deformities hidden behind stockings, closed closets,
and lonely laundry lists forever. Plant your feet firmly on the ground,
and do not hesitate to sink into the dark, cool mud, spreading
your toes across relationships and looking for love on solid ground.

Twenty-Five Years of History

When I pocketed the stray quarter on the street, I looked ahead
but not behind, so you can imagine my surprise when I heard
someone ask me my intention. I drifted back to the days you were fading,
body shutting down, limbs limp, mouth contorted into a look of wandering wonder
when I professed to you how much I would miss you, and you said, "Where are you going?"
Tonight I'm feeling like killing
his inner child—one blow to the brain—
the only thing stopping me at this point
is I no longer pass as a juvenile.
How about that punishment to follow?
How about the idea of remorse?
Seems exhausting asking these questions of myself
yet once again.

Suzanne Nielsen

Matter of Fact

"Come here," she says to me from her hospital bed.
"Closer," she says.
I bend down, inches from her face, and she tells me she has another family
living on the West Coast, three adult children, tanned and affluent, children of their own,
children who have children, none of whom know of us, her family residing in the Midwest
caring for her as she grows into her nineties. I don't know what to make of the information so
casually presented to me just above a whisper. I feel elated and cheated all at the same time,
and so I confess I have questions seeping in perspiration, coagulating under my skin, causing the vein just
right of my eye to overflow and spill a different hue of blood onto her sheets, the sheets that cover her
and protect her from scrutiny.

Pink Plugs

I waited and waited and waited some more until
I went to an audiologist. At sixty years old, I went, face-to-face
with an audiologist at the Como Clinic.
An audiologist named Seral,
or Stella, or Serial, or Surreal.
I'd paid the price in the '70s by hearing
Robert Plant say live at the St. Paul Civic Center,
"St. Paul, you're much too much."

But I couldn't much hear that now, so I went to Seral.
At the Como Clinic in St. Paul. St. Paul, who was struck blind
for three days until surrendering to the Messiah.

Two weeks later, I went back to see Seral and to pick up
my hearing aids. I'd bonded with her since our first
introduction while attempting a two-for one deal
like at the state fair. She didn't bite, but she did
something far greater.

She swung in from around the corner, gleaming with
anticipation. In her hand was a shiny, heart-shaped
box with my aids. She counted to three, uncovered
the box, and just as the doctor ordered, there in front
of me were the pinkest My Little Pony pink
metallic plugs a girl could hope for.

Suzanne Nielsen

Strolling

I notice her two-seated buggy is empty as she strolls past me
on the sidewalk crossing Colvin. Just a speck of a thing
pushing the double-wide stroller at lullaby speed,
a march to her step, hair the color of autumn flipping
atop her shoulders.

Behind her, the morning sun glares through the sycamore,
bloodred leaves ready to let go, float to the pavement
until they curl up and die. There one is now,
hesitating in flight before landing among familiarity,
forming a blanket in camaraderie.

And amidst all this quietude I hear her spew
vulgarity in rapid succession.
Some mother, I think.
I shake my head, stare at my aging hands
and consider saying something. I'm not offended,
it's not that; I'm recalling her conquest.

Yes, that's it, it's the outburst, the breaking of silence.
I'm absorbed by the intensity of the mother's expletives,
so I say, "Miss, can I comfort you?"
She stops, turns her head and says,
"Have you seen my babies this morning?"

A Mere Decade Plus Two

Twelve years have passed since I last looked seriously in the mirror; I gaze
at myself and realize my left eyebrow has turned white somewhere along the way
and I'm shorter, I do believe, than I was even yesterday. As I adjust the rearview
mirror this morning, something else draws my attention; I look beyond the mirror
and realize it is all an illusion; I will embrace the white eyebrow all the way to the
grocery store, whereupon I will purchase beets and paint my brows a lovely
cabernet that takes the plucking urge away, and red is a makeup color if there
ever was one. I watch the strangeness evolve.

Suzanne Nielsen

Bloodful Wills

Today I go to the safe deposit box
only to notice I've shrunk an inch
I can't reach up to insert my key
like I did with ease just four years ago
Louisa, the woman with the other key
to my life offers me a boost
I tell her I'm here to make a few changes
to my will
"Without a lawyer?" she asks.
Who needs a lawyer when my handwriting is legible?
She leaves me alone, so I scratch lines
through old promises
like how I said I'd leave my
book of poems to R.T. Tin
my favorite torn slippers to Lassie
my favorite literary magazines and books to their descendants
Until I found out R.T. Tins were sporting Chins
Lassie's Newfoundlands
and Pekinese landed in Pomerania
far-off descendants of both Lassie and Mr. Tin.
I'm too old for this blending of the bloods.

Face Up

I see on Facebook that my birth mother has died.
I look at her photo, the size of a postage stamp, and there
in the background are several of her adult
children. Nothing alphabetically chronological in names,
more of a focus on birth order.

I slip back forty years, and there I am in the middle of a
snowstorm. My wiper blades have no protection,
metal on glass fighting metal on ice. I need to get to
where I'm going. So I drive peering through little
20/20 slits in the windshield determined to find her, them,
the family that was left behind. Their
neighbors insist I ran away. Others were told I was
institutionalized. Still others were suspicious, but kept
to themselves. I was three at the time, my god, sixty years
ago.

There stands a woman on the corner of Cedar and
Seventh smoking, nothing covering her head, her
hands chapped, I see. She speaks in a low growl. Asks me
if I am she, the girl that got away.
Before I answer she pulls out of her pocket an over-
worked billfold, opens it and headshots of strangers
litter the pavement, some curious enough to land face-
first.
These are my children, she says.
I think we are playing gin rummy, trying to match faces in
pairs.
Some are duplicates, she says.
She bends over, stands wide and gathers her collection,

rambling rampantly.
Kathy, Anita, Phyllis, Evelyn, Lawrence, and Amy. Those
are your sisters and brother. That's your family.
Now we have to find Michael. You look good, are your
mom and dad good to you?
I stopped her at that point. I saw where this was going.
Five years from now. Ten years from now. Twenty
years from now.

Forty years from now
far away, removed.

I see on Facebook that my birth mother has died.
I look at her photo, the size of a postage stamp, and there
in the background are several of her adult
children. Nothing alphabetically chronological in names,
more of a focus on birth order. Or not. Skipping
the oldest. Skipping the third child, yet keeping duplicates
like wild cards, keeping things orderly, keeping
the curious at bay.

Bridge to Heaven

God looks down and sighs
as dust covers the scene
and waters make way for
the weight of the city's despair.

Repair stands stunned off in the distance
as Robin Trower plays his Stratocaster
and Hendrix chimes in from the heavens above
providing a bridge back for those who mourn.

Raining from Heaven

The birds congregate on 694 and 61 every morning
to let go of old resentments and figure out their next
major move. Routes are plotted in advance like tours
of duty. These are the birds that don't fly south but
weather the storms of a barbaric Minnesota winter.
These are the birds that snitch on the albino squirrel who
empties the feeders on the entire block of Edmund
Avenue
while the birds resume congregating and dreaming of seedlings
raining from heaven.

Reading Lips

It started off slowly, or perhaps it was my hesitancy at
recognizing that something had changed. Something that I
had feared would leave its mark since age seven, when I
pressed
to my ear the large stone from the oven wrapped in a
fuzzy pink towel,
hoping the ache would crawl out and creep away, but for
years the ache
returned, each time leaving behind scars omitting the "s"
sound.

So I stayed keenly alert to the movement of lips. Yes, the
movement of their
lips at the Lowell Inn on my golden birthday, and they
kept asking if I wanted
scalloped potatoes or string beans or horseradish for my
tenderloin,
and all of this I pick up through a sonar device behind the
bridge of my nose.

I left the dining area and followed the waves, joined the
dancing dolphins,
and once we established territorial lines we swam side by
side, me feeding them
string beans, them teaching me a language of pure and
pulsed sounds, a language
engulfed to most mammals who listen.

Suzanne Nielsen

Minnesota Heat

I can't wear a tank top because my top has tanked. It's the seventh day
in a row where the temp has steadied in the nineties, and the heat index
in Moorhead is 134. I'm a Minnesotan. Born and raised. I've never lived
outside this blue state. The summers in Minnesota are deadly. Horrid, torrential.

Especially when your tits die and you slide into surgery. Let bygones be,
I know, but I'm a tank topper, or I was a tank topper until the compressions, the
same compressions that left me gasping for air for days after. The compressions
that sank in sweat for seven days in a row. OSHA recommends a degree range
between 68 and 78 degrees.

There are no windows on the north side of the house, there's no air conditioning.
This is the house I inherited when my Depression parents passed on. The air is stale
and no longer transparent. Everything hangs in mist and OSHA would suggest traveling
north. Duluth, Lake Superior, but I can't move my arms. I can't sleep except in a sitting
position. My compressions are two inches thick so I cannot see what I look like.

I cannot lift my head because I'm literally deflated and my sweat weighs heavy
within the confines. No sudden movements welcome, no bigger the better the
tighter the sweater chest exercises for me. I just sit here and wait for the fireflies
to appear. Then I will fall asleep while reading
Letters of Samuel Rutherford.

Moonglow

She said she wanted to return to that special place
she visited so long ago where the giraffe spoke French
and the dolphin sang bitter blues to a keyboard playing
in the background and where she remembered once on a still night
the phosphorescence danced in response to her lead.
But how to get back, where is there?
Follow the stars falling across the moon.

Mental Health Update

I don't get a warning, it's not like a gunshot goes off and I drop to the floor. For days I climb into bed wearing my street clothes that haven't seen the streets for weeks. I smell myself like a dog, numb to the disgust because this is what it's like living with an invisible disease that sucks the marrow out of your bones.

By day four I make myself go to the grocery store during senior hour.
I am home, unpacked by 7:35 a.m., and cigarettes don't taste good
with lukewarm coffee. It's an effort to smoke so I lug my limbs
back to bed while my mind writes stories with no endings.
I want to become invisible.

Yes, I'm trolling for the magic cloak on eBay covered in soft sage
velour to be my one and only sedative to shroud me from intruders
who maniacally make their way to the finish line, the ending
of the story only to recognize that it's recursive.

Suzanne Nielsen

Your Gut Response

You can't enter a story with dialogue;
there's no grounding to where we are, no backbone to
what's been happening.
You don't know the first thing about writing a story, I tell her
in the kitchen as she prepares the grocery list alphabetically
always starting with basil.
Never enough basil.
Followed by Captain Crunch and cigarettes.
Then write a story about how basil doesn't talk, she screams
over the grinding of the garbage disposal.
The kitchen reeks of ground leaves, sour milk, and stale smoke.
Write a story about a humming refrigerator,
a half-filled glass or the wrath of it being half empty, she says,
because no story should start with dialogue.

News and a Cigarette

She said he had wild eyes,
the man across the hall.
Made his hair, or lack of, more noticeable.
Made her chew the inside of her mouth
until she'd taste the raw red metal
skin hidden within the cave
of her hollow cheek.
At 6:57 each morning
when his door opened
to retrieve the morning paper
she'd sneak a look out her peephole
at his unshaven face, cigarette dangling
from the right corner of his mouth,
his bent torso in a torn undershirt
where the ribs of his frame stuck out
like bare branches on a tree.
He bent to touch a pair of beige boots
with tattered lining, tipped each one upside down,
first the left, then the right,
waiting for the other foot to fall,
smoldered squinted eyes stared,
he returned through the door from which he came,
empty-handed because the paper was never delivered.

Empty Is a State of Mind

There was something odd
about the brightness
in that white-walled room,
something odd indeed in contrast
to the black night fading, the frame of
the bed left leaning up against the open window,
the uniting of the black and white
extension cords reminded her
to bleed the radiator
and listen for his sigh.

Face Painting

Never put a face with a name,
that's where pathos reels peep shows
a peekaboo encumbrance that expires
one's own imagination to the point of
adding airbrush touches to barren branches.

Never put a lamp on a street corner,
that attracts infringing wings forcing
a nuisance hum, an unhummable
humdrum humbug *humph* to the human,
leaving a nocturnal scenario that slaps you silly.

Never put your work on the internet,
that's where noms de plume exist for a reason,
the reason being no one is left responsible,
just the nomadic nomenclature signaling
a face with many names but no signatures.

Never put a rhubarb patch on public property,
that will come back to haunt you and before you can make
jam, you will be in a jam with no rhyme or reason
wishing good riddance to the idea of anonymity
and severing the roots of the annihilator.

With all these nevers, will you ever find a nerve
that doesn't twitch at the slightest unnerving or
a face without a name or a story without a writer
or a writer without a story shamelessly living in
the depths of cyberspace, building a fire?

Suzanne Nielsen

Enter to Win a Trip to Las Vegas

I follow the signs
labyrinthine
leading to what's
a "humongous"
garage sale
while the radio talks of
Aladdin's paranoia
over the favorable mention
by Ronstadt of Moore.

She's soon to embark on
America's social security
soon to live with assurance
of capitalistic health insurance
she's sold more records
than Kate Smith
a Woodstock woman
who never lost a beat
makes me want to beat up someone
instead I stop at the humongous sale
grab a fifty-cent sweatshirt
with "see hear say no evil" imprinted on the front
then reach for an
"authentic Voodoo Doll from Mexico,"
$1.00.

I dig into my pocket, pull out six quarters
imprinted with liberty
hand them over and head to my car
wondering

Face Up

how did I get here?
How far to Tijuana?

Atom and Eve

When you hear that gas is unaffordable
the thought of growing gas seems
like a sensible alternative so at 7:12 p.m.
on Friday evening you walk out the door
in search of gas bulbs to plant
gas grapes to turn into wine
gas windows to shield you from the
masks needed to bury
your Chrysler underneath
the harvested pumpkin patch
where nitrates wait to be charged.

Blue Noise

When you wake up and your email says
    Good day.
    Satan always finds mischief for idle hands.
    Journalists belong in the gutter because that is where
    the ruling classes throw their guilty secrets.
    There are times when one would like to hang the whole
    human race, and end the farce.
    Not the fruit of experience but experience itself is the
    end.
It's time to write
endlessly
so others
don't believe they control
the volume.
Or worse,
that Satan's evil fruit
will go bad in your crisper.

Suzanne Nielsen

True Identities

I walked through the graveyard this morning, and Isabella
Durant spoke to me from down under.
She said she'd made a deal with God that permitted her
to visit three people three times over the
course of thirty years. For three decades, she glimpsed in
on her two children and an ex-lover.

The ex-lover had aged poorly, leaving him a bad speller by
the first decade, diabetic the second, and
obsolete the third. Her two sons, on the other hand,
displayed minimal wear, and yet their faces
revealed inbred tension and fear. Maybe it was a
camouflaged fabric they used to hide their true
identities, disengaged looks directed at passersby,
slashing a moral compass and infringing on public
disobedience.

Why had her sons hardened? Then she remembered all
the times she told them to shut up, to leave her
be, to be seen and not heard, to be rock solid, and to
serve others as self-sacrifice.

Isabella warned me that through our exchange she would
soon be cut off, she would leave this world
and journey into the unknown where silence rules and
darkness prevails.

When I returned home, I called my children and begged
them to confront their fears; I called my ex-lover
and told him to drop the phonics if he knew what was

good for him. Then I contemplated my life in three decades hoping when all is said and done a quiet place will welcome me where I will spell words like vernacular and iridescent.

Suzanne Nielsen

Have a Home

Have a home had a home want a home paint a home repair a home
shame a home burn a home apologize to home leave a home alone
but empty its contents carry a flashlight matches a deed a need
to return to the closet where two wire hangers with slender
shoulders escape beneath the floorboards.

Translocation

Geese were about yesterday for within two miles
I'd counted seventeen, a group of eight flying in an almost uniform V,
a group of five flying in a row, four more following behind
at different speeds. One in the road flattened
with its wing perched up toward the sky.

Later that evening I am standing in line outside
a theater, thinking about smoking, when a student I'd
had in a writing class approaches me. I hadn't seen her
in many years. Names don't always come to me, but if I think back
to what someone has written I can usually recall the name,
such was the case.
I asked if she was still writing.
I told her she looked happy.
She told me two weeks earlier she'd had surgery.
Her partner needed a kidney, and hers matched perfectly.
Two weeks ago? I said. And look at you, who would know?
Our eyes locked, and for a brief moment I saw in the reflection of her
eyeglasses my new haircut, in the shape of a kidney.

You saved your partner's life, I said, drifting back to the street,
back into the evening chill and the hum of the traffic.
Oh no, she said. He saved mine when he encouraged me to write.
Off she walked, but as I watched, I saw her wings spread
and take flight.

Suzanne Nielsen

Tree House

That last vertebra shows bark on bark,
leaving the arthritic condition of the
lower limbs just a bit too exposed
to the testimonies of a spring bloom.
Now your frame houses starlings,
red squirrels, and the Jacobsons' Siamese
during hours the half moon
flies, fourteen nights before rain.

Another American Invasion

She sits at the kitchen table, watching the evening news,
when the telephone rings. The phone screen says it's a call
coming from her son, a Green Beret. She lights a cigarette,
waiting for another American invasion.

He'd deployed to the Mideast three times in the last five years,
surviving a gunshot to the heart. She visited him after the war
wound, where she traced the scarred shrapnel of his chest armor
while the smell of machine-gun fire singed her nose hairs.

He'd sent her a phone video of his living arrangement, captured
on screen such shiny granite countertops, blue skies through the
skylight's vertical window shades in a restful color of sand.
When did the lying start?

She lights another cigarette while the phone rings in the background.
The cloud of smoke she exhales forms the shape of a grenade. A grenade
powerful enough to leave behind shadows of memory that soon evaporate.
She gets up, turns off the television and vows to see her son's body as whole,

no scars, no shrapnel embedded, and to feel the restful
color of sand.

Consequences of Dawn

Looking for something to stop
the need for longing is essential for the woman
in the black overcoat, whose hands fumble
the loose tobacco and silver change in her deep pockets.
It's not in finding what's lost,
it's in the discovery that she's found
a window opening the dawn of a new day;
at least that's what she tells herself as she
traces the lines of the blue blanket left
crumpled among saffron slivers of light.

Suzanne Nielsen

Such Colorful Stories

I develop plots until she falls asleep, slight grin on her face. I pull the blankets up to her chin,
startling her awake. "Sit down and tell me a story," she says in a sixty-six-year-old voice, spirit
drifting, "I'm not going to make it, so be quick about it. Get to the plot, get to the end."
She traces my fingers with her jagged nails, and I suggest a home manicure.

I gather the colored bottles off the windowsill and paint with pastels. "Such a fuss for
me?" She shuts her eyes and sighs. As I brush each nail a different color, I think back
to eight years old, her blowing my nails dry with Dentyne breath. So pretty, she'd say.
"Shake your hands like this," she'd say, wagging her wrists in circles.

I paint for far too long, into the night and the dawn of the next day. As I steady the brush
I continue with my story while the sun hits her lids. She lifts her head from the pillow
while her nails tip-toe across her wrinkled hospital sheet and says, "So many colors.
You've given me a rainbow to look at. It's like magic. Such colorful stories."

"Do you want to know the ending?" I ask. She squishes up her face, and I know she knows
that I know the ending has entered the room. So pale.

Face Up

Open the window, shroud the clock,
let the pastels dance on the window's ledge.

Filling My Mother's Shoes

My mother wore heels to bed. Size 9. Medium width. She wore heels every day of her life, even when
she and my father'd go fishing on the great northern lakes of Minnesota the third week of August. Not
flashy heels by any means. Mostly muted taupes, browns, and variations of black. Occasionally she'd
move into red hues, but not often. She was not a proponent of polishing shoes, only wearing them.

How could she sleep in heels, you might ask. Since I can remember, she and my father have slept in
different corners of the house. The Pomeranian shared her bed with her for six years, but avoided her
feet, always curled up on the satin pillow next to her head.

The thing I remember most about the size 9s was the perpetual sound of being under construction. The bungalow-style house we lived in had bare maple floors throughout with the exception of vinyl floor
covering in the bathroom and kitchen. In high school I moved into the basement, away from the yipping
dog and heavy smell of Opium cologne. The hammering of the heels echoed through the floorboards
until the black nights faded to gray mornings, seven days a week. Following the hammering was a trail of
clickity-clicks, the sound cards make stuck in the spokes of your bike wheels. That was the Pomeranian,
dutifully following her around.

Face Up

She never slept much. One day she discovered her leg had swollen and her heeled shoe was permanently planted on her left foot. This was the beginning of a series of unfortunate events.

Nine months later, my mother lay in a hospital bed spitting up muted blood. Her feet were bare, swollen and blue. I was shuffling cards for my next game of solitaire. A week earlier I had watched a team of medical professionals hold my mother down as they gently made incisions along the sides of her leather shoe and lifted it off her foot. It was as though she was giving birth through cesarean, and the fetus was stillborn. That was the day she unwillingly surrendered her dignity and her mind turned to Jell-O.

For a moment in time, the shuffling of the cards sprang her back into action. "Where's my shoes?" she said. "In your closet," I answered. A red 7 on a black 8, the luck of an ace, click, click, click. "Get them and put them on my feet." I walked over to the closet in my rubber-soled Doc Martens and reached inside for the pair that she had worn walking into the hospital just seven days earlier. The left shoe mutilated and deformed, like her foot now naked. "Let me see," she said, holding her hands out to grab the shoes from me. "Did Sy chew this up like this?" "Must have," I said. "Nasty little dog," she said.

I worked the shoes, shoving her swollen feet into their confines. She was the princess of the ball, and she was late to get home.

Suzanne Nielsen

Forty Percent Lost

Three years ago, I sent away for my DNA results. It was a twofer deal;
I kept playing their jingle in my mind, "Know the world from the inside,
discover where your family is without leaving your living room."
Before COVID, this seemed enticing. I broke out the plastic and got my twofer
deal despite my husband's grimace. My Scottish husband wears plaid, and I
wanted to get to the bottom of it. Me, on the other hand, being adopted,
my DNA was a crapshoot.

By the time our results arrived, I'd forgotten what piqued my interest. I left
the envelope on the counter, and, once again, forgot about it until three days
later my husband said, "I'm Nigerian." I looked at him through squinty
eyes and admitted I'd grown accustomed to the plaid. "What does yours say?"
he asked following me from the kitchen to the living room to ice the orchids.

It made him itchy that I wouldn't read my results so he read them to me. "Twenty-nine percent
Italian. Ha! That explains a lot," he said. I grabbed the papers from him and read on.

"Tell me the rest," he said, as he paced back and forth with his hand on his chin, a
Yorubian trait. "Thirty-one percent mishmash," I said, ripping up the evidence, tossing it in the
trash on top of moldy marinara sauce. Like my orchids, I'm a hybrid unrecognizable
mess, but that's a mouthful to say so instead I looked out the window.
"How about the rest?" he insisted. As though he needed reassurance.
"I'm forty percent lost," I muttered as I walked back to admire the orchids.

Hoops

Just when you think the hoops to jump through
are filled with butter crème, the dossier you worked
six months assembling, birthing it for years
like a litter of letters, isn't enough at face value.

Now you have to scan the fucker,
over five hundred pages, so you can send
it electronically during COVID.
You're stupid.
It's a week before your committee
deliberates on your future, your promotion
and tenure in order to prove you're worthy of
doing what you've been paid to do for twenty-two
years.

Simultaneously Fed Ex gets three hundred
dollars for their pain-in-the-ass scanning.
Does my committee get a payback?
Twenty-two years of teaching
face to face
is nothing compared to an
electronic version of what you do.

Excuse Me

I can't find my youth. I face the change, subtle like a slap in the face,
perhaps influenced by the pandemic, I lack an interest in what I wear.

Just like Aunt Lillian when she aged. Her liver-spotted hands a radiant glow of drug-store foundation just a shade darker
than need be and age is just a number.

Across the room, excuse me! Those are my fingers clutching a bouquet,
a nervous hitch in my smile, corn silk hair, wearing white bright white,
ready to trip down the aisle, ready to make this one of the most memorable days of my life.

followed by several trips down the aisle. But me, looking In, looking on. Waiting for the trip
to twirl to the next to the next to the more than four, almost five decades, and Aunt Lill has been gone
almost as long. A life ago I thought those flowers would live forever.

Suzanne Nielsen

Thirty-Seven Seconds

Yesterday I braved a visit to my local coffeehouse
where I sat masked in the corner and listened to the
woman behind me talk about her woes as a school bus
driver. They schlep in everything from pet centipedes to
their dad's weed prescription, she says. I have a rule, she
says. I refuse to wait any longer than thirty-seven seconds
for a student
to get on the bus. Any longer, and I'm late. I'm late, I get
written
up, I get written up, I get canned. Where am I gonna get
another
job with narcolepsy?

Welcome to my world of invisible demons who invade
our lowly little minds and put us to sleep at the height of a
career, those invisible demons that direct us into the ring
where the matador swings his red cape into the final act,
a muleta pierces my aorta and I'm tired, I'm very
very tired, too tired to ride the bus so I wait for
another story to slip into, another thirty-seven seconds.

Profile of a Poet

The sepia's fading as I get closer to a T in the road where I see
my sixty-something self staring at the carpet lines, the shadow of my
footprints, the weight of the lead in my legs, and I realize that place
I'm talking about, that place on Devil's Hill where I nurtured numb,
where I picked up the horsehair brush and stroked my mother's
mane one hundred times while she cried about her marriage.

I see snapshots of defeat as I rewind the decades,
a true bricoleur with a lifeguard certification who stood stoic
at the water's edge as a man fled into the frigid waters one early
March afternoon, the sun starting its descent, his bobbing head
hallowed, his words reassuring me that this is his moment of
glory as he goes under the third and final time.

I climb Devil's Hill nurturing numb. Perhaps the one hundred strokes made her
think of happier moments; perhaps there was a moment of glory lurking
in the depths of March waters. Psych wards, nursing homes, halfway houses,

Suzanne Nielsen

my neighbor downstairs already drunk at noon, my
defenseless cat I declawed
four months earlier. I think of the bridge of my nose
widening with age, my laugh
lines deepening. I trace my flamboyant forehead, my
mother's mane, and the sepia
returns. Has all this taken place in just one lifetime?

Acknowledgments

The publication of *Face Up* was made possible by a generous donation from General Mills. Without this financial support, Oleb Books would have not been able to hire all of the publishing professionals involved in the book production process, as well as create accessible file formats for the title. Thank you, General Mills!

About the Author

Suzanne Nielsen's *Face Up* is the winner of the 2021 Oleb Books Poetry Prize. Nielsen is also the author of *I Think You Should Know* (So'ham Books). Her poetry, fiction, and essays have appeared in literary journals nationally and internationally; some of these include *Identity Theory*, *The Pedestal*, *Word Riot*, and *580 Split*. She is an associate professor of creative writing at Metropolitan State University in the Twin Cities of Minnesota. When she is not writing or grading papers, she can be found hanging out with her menagerie of rescue cats and dogs in her St. Paul home. Learn more at olebbooks.com/suzanne-nielsen.

www.ingramcontent.com/pod-product-compliance
Lightning Source LLC
Chambersburg PA
CBHW071912070526
44583CB00016B/1959